Deschutes
Public Library

S0-AKR-833

NOVOGRATZ
DESIGN FIX

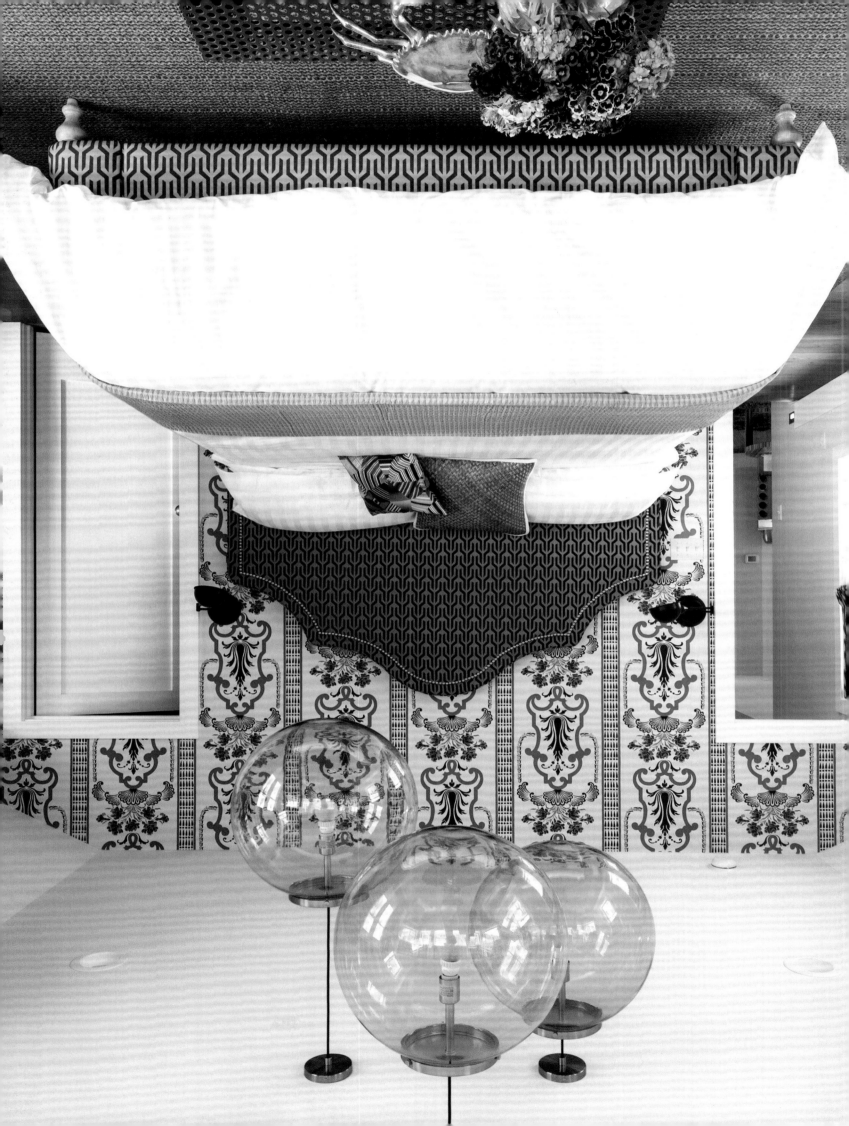

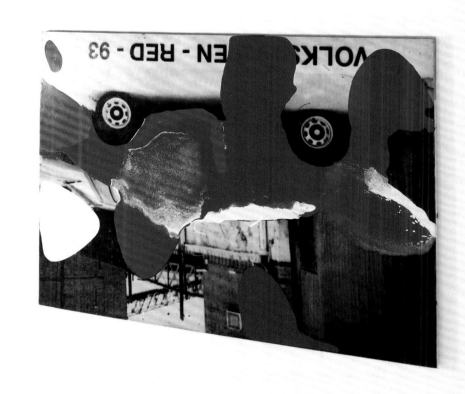

NOVOGRATZ
DESIGN FIX

Chic and Stylish Tips for Every Decorating Scenario

ROBERT AND CORTNEY NOVOGRATZ
WITH ELIZABETH NOVOGRATZ

FOREWORD BY INDIA HICKS

RIZZOLI
NEW YORK

New York · Paris · London · Milan

CONTENTS

FOREWORD

INDIA HICKS

I can't quite remember how we met, but I knew I wanted to meet them. They headed up a design empire, traveled the world, lived like gypsies and like kings, worked their arses off and had seven kids. Seven. SEVEN.

But I suspect if you are reading this you already know this, because they have published several books, had their own TV show, toured across the country, and shared a lot on social media. And I am so happy they have done all of this because we all need someone to look up to. I only have five kids. Compared to this dynamic duo, I'm not even trying.

I might not remember how we met, but I remember when we met. It was a warm evening in LA, they had invited us to dinner—in their crazy castle-house in the hills. Rather like a blind date, none of us knew what to expect. Within minutes my kids were scattered amongst theirs, skateboarding, ping-ponging, drumming—and not just in your normal bottom-of-the-basement kind of drumming but in an uber-cool-designer-padded-room kind of drumming.

David Flint Wood, my partner, and Robert sat outside under the stars, at a long trestle table, drinking tall inviting drinks beside an open fire as the smell of orange and olive trees drifted by. Cortney whisked me into the kitchen—all wooden floors, steel doors and marble surfaces. I loved it, but what I loved even more was that she had not cooked dinner. Someone else had. Thank god, that would have been the end of a new friendship. You can't live in a castle you've designed, mother seven kids, run a business AND cook dinner for your blind date.

Our friendship grew. Cortney included me in get-togethers and other outings whenever she could. And when I was painfully winding down my own lifestyle brand and closing my LA office, Cortney arranged a girl's night out to have drinks in the city's newest, most sought-after hotspot, and afterwards to a comedy club to cheer me up. It just so happened that our third friend got hit by a car on her way into the show. Not very funny. She was OK—just a little bruised and very shocked. But looking back, the evening was a reflection of everything "Novogratz": thoughtfulness, style, and, always, the unexpected.

INTRODUCTION

ROBERT AND CORTNEY NOVOGRATZ

We can't believe this is our fourth book and our third published by Rizzoli. What makes this book different from the others we've done is that it is mostly a compilation of projects that we designed for other people (of course, we included a few of our own homes too). All of the projects in this book are new, aside from our country house in Great Barrington, Massachusetts. We redo it every few years and included it to showcase the latest updates and renovations.

Our two biggest projects to date are the Hollywood Hills "castle" (Chapter One) and the townhouse on the West Side Highway in New York City's West Village (Chapter Two). Sadly, both homes have since been sold, but the show must go on. The projects that we designed for clients range from a 300-square-foot bungalow in San Diego to a huge family beach house in Bellport, Long Island.

These days people are living less traditionally and we love it. The projects in this book have taken us all over the country, and have broadened the scope of our work to include a prefabricated house in Montauk, New York, a starter home in Silver Lake, Los Angeles, a boutique hotel in Woodstock, New York, and a house built and designed with the ever-growing short-term rental market in mind (i.e., Airbnb) in Seabrook, Washington.

Airbnb and other rental services have become a way of life for many, and they are here to stay. Chapter Three and the Resources section in the back of the book offer lots of tips on how to organize your home when you're hosting short-term renters.

No matter who you are or what your lifestyle is, there are tips, ideas, and inspiration for you in this book. We designed for singles, newly married couples, people who've been together for decades, large families, empty nesters, renters, owners, surfers, art lovers, book collectors, antiques aficionados, sports fans, flea market junkies, minimalists, and hoarders. We included homes that deal with every type of budget and that are located everywhere, from overlooking the ocean to the middle of the woods. The projects live all over the USA—they are in small towns, the middle of the country, and of course, more than one happens to be in our favorite city on Earth, New York.

We had a blast putting this book together. We hope you have as much fun following along as we did designing the spaces.

"Tip the world over
on its side and
everything loose
will land in "

—Frank Lloyd Wright

CHAPTER ONE

THIS OLD HOLD

HOLLYWOOD HILLS, LOS ANGELES

GOALS

1   To transform a large 100-year-old house with a byzantine floor plan into an open family home with a good flow from room to room.

2   To make the house feel more intimate yet retain the classic (i.e., a little dramatic!) Hollywood Hills style.

3   To build a private outdoor oasis in the middle of urban Los Angeles.

4   To add multiple spaces for entertainment, including a game room, music room, home theater, and bar.

CHALLENGES

→ **A poorly designed floor plan:** There were hallways and staircases everywhere creating a confining—and confusing—layout, so we opened up the entire space by knocking down several interior walls. We converted 7 small bedrooms into 4 larger ones. We moved the living areas to the main floor and the bedrooms and other spaces that were used less often to the floors above and below.

→ **Replacing multiple layers of flooring:** The house had many different types of flooring that had been laid over the years. We got rid of all of them and replaced all the hardwood flooring with reclaimed oak floors from Germany to create a better flow.

→ **Remodeling a shabby entryway:** The original front door to the home entered straight into the kitchen area. It felt anticlimactic and took away from the grandeur of the house. We added a gated entrance as a second means of egress which felt more elegant and provided more privacy.

→ **Bad windows:** The windows were a mix throughout: Some were made with great old steel frames and others had aluminum subpar frames and there were a few made from wood. Unfortunately, the beautiful steel windows needed to be reglazed (to ensure they met current building codes) which was as expensive as replacing them, so we sold them, which offset the costs of the expensive steel windows we used throughout the entire property. It was our largest investment in the home and worth every penny.

→ **Retaining the original character and integrity of a 1920s house while still doing a gut renovation:** One of the keys to striking this delicate balance was by restoring the facade to its original aesthetic, a white and black color scheme. We were also able to save the circular staircase, the rotunda ceiling, and the original front door.

→ **Bad roof:** The house had many different roof lines and a number of turrets that were unattractive. We replaced the entire roof with a grey slate shingled roof, which gave it a uniform look.

→ **Lack of privacy:** Because of the short distance between the street and the door—which is typical for houses in Los Angeles—we added Sunbrella fabric to the front gates to create a more private front and planted high hedges all around the property as soon as we bought it. By the time we started construction, they'd already grown enough to enclose the yard.

After 20 years of living in Manhattan, and one too
many brutal winters, we packed up our 7 kids and
headed across the country. We moved our brood
from the West Village in New York City to the
Hollywood Hills.

We arrived in August, a week before the school
year began. We quickly moved into a rental home, and
immediately began to scour the city in search of the
perfect fixer-upper. We had some important criteria
as we began the search: As New Yorkers, a home
within walking distance to restaurants and city life was
non-negotiable. But we also wanted to take advantage
of the incredible California weather, which meant an
outdoor space with a big patio and a swimming pool.

It didn't take long. After searching for a few weeks,
we found the house of our dreams. It was also cen-
trally located to the 4 different schools we'd enrolled
the kids in, because it would have been too easy to
put them all in the same school (why make things
easy for ourselves, not our style!). More importantly,
it was right up the hill from the legendary Chateau
Marmont hotel.

The home was an old castle that had been built in
the 1920s by a silent film star. Remarkably, there had
been only 3 owners in 100 years, but all 3 clearly had
very different tastes from one another, which was
now our problem to contend with. There were many
small rooms, many types of hardwood flooring, and a
nonsensical floor plan. The house felt like a maze with
tiny rooms and multiple doorways that led to more
doorways and even more tiny rooms. Everything had
to be gutted and redone. In other words, it was perfect.

Our biggest challenge was to keep the charm and
period feel of the house while modernizing the entire
space. We opened everything up to give the space a
loftlike look and created a seamless feel between the
indoors and outdoors.

The open living room, with views
of the Hollywood Hills from every
window.

FLEA MARKET FINDS: WHAT TO LOOK FOR

- ↝ Quirky decorative objects: Look for whatever speaks to you. If you love it and can afford it, bring it home.
- ↝ Someone else's family heirlooms: Other people's loot will bring history, mystery, and personality to a shelf or table.
- ↝ Small furniture: a fun chair or colorful end table can change the entire feel of a room. It can become a focal point or perk up a dull area of the house.
- ↝ Interesting lighting and lamps: Lamps are easy and inexpensive to rewire, so don't worry about whether or not it works. The only question is, "Will it bring life to the space"?
- ↝ Inexpensive but interesting art: The question you should ask yourself is not "Is it good?" but rather "Do I love it?"

TIPS FOR A BETTER FLEA MARKET EXPERIENCE

↪ Always get there at dawn or as soon as they open—the best pieces always go fast and early.

↪ The best vendors are usually in the front, right in the middle of everything, so start there.

↪ Bring cash as most vendors don't take checks and many still don't have credit card machines.

↪ We pay quickly if it's something we love because most of the time, it won't be there if we leave and come back.

↪ After we purchase something, we leave it with the seller until we are ready to go home. If this is your MO as well, a word to the wise: take a photo of the booth number as we have spent hours trying to find the booth at the end of the day and sometimes even forgot a piece or two.

MIXING HIGH AND LOW: ESSENTIALS FOR THE NOVOGRATZ STYLE

We've been incorporating a mix of high and low decorative elements and furnishings into our designs since the early days. We had to make the most of our small budgets so we got creative and fell in love with all the amazing finds at flea markets, garage sales, and roadside antique stores. Incorporating flea market items into our projects started out as a necessity, and now it's an essential part of our style. We recognized early on that furniture and accessories from these sources brought a lot of fun into a space, made a room or home less serious, more interesting, and most importantly, made it personal.

We began to add art into our designs as soon as we could afford to. In many projects, we spend a good portion of the budget on art and less on furniture as we believe these pieces will increase in value more than a couch or chair. Buying inexpensive art is easier than ever, which wasn't true when we first started designing houses.

FLEA MARKETS

Back when we were getting started, during the early morning hours on Saturdays and Sundays, while our friends would still be out partying, we'd wake up before dawn and head out to the flea markets all over New York City and up and down the East Coast. We've kept up that tradition for 25 years.

Many of our favorite pieces, antiques, and fun decorative items tell the stories of our time scouring the fleas. Over the years, our knowledge has grown and we have more to spend, but the fun and excitement remains the same. You never know what you'll find. Even if you don't buy anything, it's always a fun day to walk around, people-watch, and be inspired.

OPPOSITE: Another view of the living room and the dining room perfectly illustrates our high/low style: Tom Dixon prototype orange chair (high); pale blue salvaged chairs (purchased at a flea market and reupholstered—low); and decorative objects on the coffee table are all from flea markets (low).

"Style is something very individual, very personal, and in their own unique way, I believe **EVERYONE IS STYLISH.**"

—**Salman Khan**

TIPS FOR BETTER BOOKSHELVES

→ Incorporate decorative items such as action figures, keepsakes, photographs, and art.

→ Arrange books by color or size.

→ Shelve the books in horizontal stacks to create a fun look.

→ Add plants—a little bit of green is always a good thing.

→ Stay away from staged books, wrapped in paper.

OPPOSITE: The blending of interesting objects, heirlooms, photos, and books on a library shelf is an affordable way to create a space in the room that has personality and life. Let the books be the main feature, as a beautiful book is timeless, elegant and affordable, and use the decorative items to bring color, humor, and variety. Bookshelves should evolve over time—collections don't just come together in a single day, so be patient.

ABOVE: Somehow that Tom Ford book ends up in every library we ever come across.

FOLLOWING PAGES: The dining room with the living room in the background.

"Who ever said that PLEASURE wasn't FUNCTIONAL?"
—**Charles Eames**

In many properties we've come across, we've discovered hidden windows that have been boarded or covered up. In the original castle, there were two closets in the dining room that covered two old windows. We tore down the closets and opened the space so that those two windows became part of the main room.

The black steel windows were a big expense but we feel that they make the house. We used black steel hardware for the window treatments to match the windows and give the home a seamless, classic look.

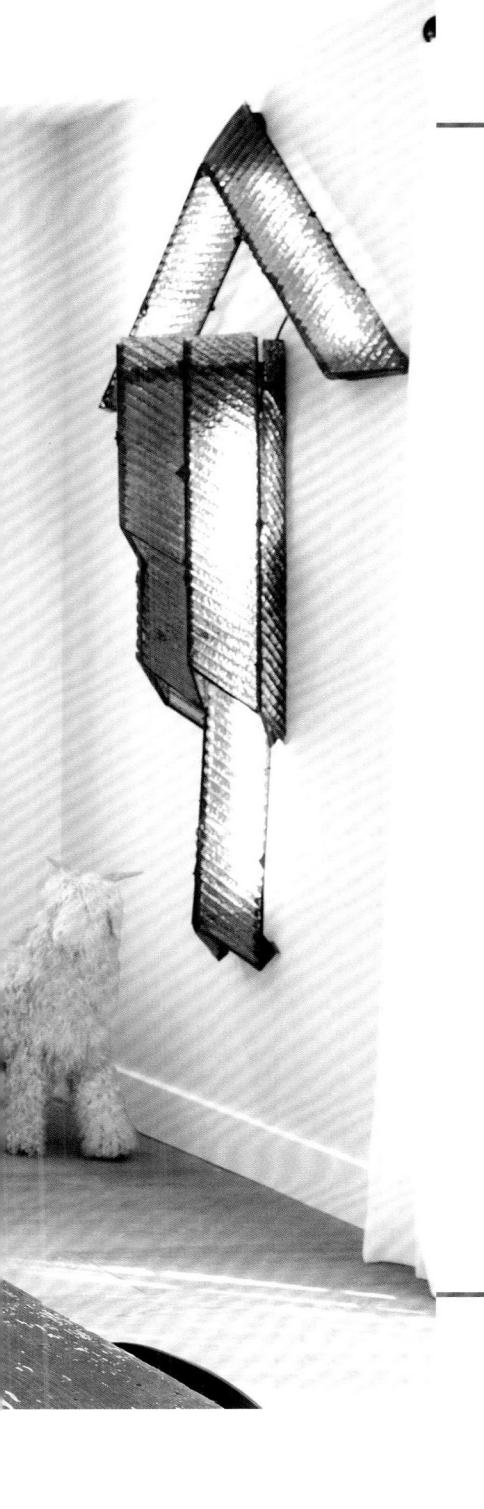

TIPS FOR CREATING AN OPEN FLOOR PLAN

→ All non-structural walls are easy to remove. Determining whether or not a wall is structural is as simple as a knock on the wall to feel the density—does it sound hollow or not? If you are still unsure, then you'll need to open the wall to see if it is a load-bearing, or structural, wall.

→ Structural walls have to be replaced by steel beams, which are much more costly, so those walls should only be removed if it's an absolute necessity or cost is not an issue.

→ Paint can make a space feel expansive or cramped. Using one color throughout makes the space feel bigger and more cohesive. Colors like grey, navy blue, white, or even black are considered more classic and have a high-end effect. For smaller spaces like bedrooms, we prefer to use different shades of red, green, orange, pink, and yellow.

→ We added hardwood floors throughout, even in the kitchen, so all the rooms feel connected.

→ Design the room so that you can see it from the entire space. Take note where the best natural light is coming from, and whether it's from a large window or from French doors.

→ Let more light in by enlarging a window or doorway.

→ Higher ceilings will open the space even more. Raising the ceilings is not easy nor is it even possible in most projects. But if and when it's doable, and we can steal 6 inches in the beams, or add a couple of feet from an unused attic or storage space above the room, we do it. For this house, we managed to do away with the large attic above the master bedroom, which made an enormous difference in how the room feels.

ABOVE: The salvaged dining room table.

FOLLOWING PAGES: The kitchen table, with a wall of art behind it. This is a great example of how we mix high and low: One of the artworks, *Get Paid*, is by Mark Bradford, which we purchased at a benefit auction for several thousand dollars, while the Abe Lincoln artwork was $50.

The kitchen had the lowest ceilings in the house, and we couldn't raise them, so we kept it minimal, white, and open to make the room feel more spacious. When in doubt, white is always the solution to make a space feel larger.

Every job we do starts with a budget and a wish list. In the past, the kitchen and bath have been our priorities. They were up there on the list for this house as well, but the windows and doors took priority. Whether you are planning to flip a property, sell it eventually, or stay forever, we think resale is something that should always be kept in mind.

WHERE WE $PLURGED

→ The Torrance Steel windows and doors were quite expensive. We felt they were an important investment, as they made the house elegant and distinct. If you love the look yet can't afford it, you can use steel on the main doorway and mimic the rest in aluminum and or even do aluminum throughout.

→ The reclaimed wood floors were the second most expensive item on our wish list. These were quite expensive but are incredibly durable and well-made and get better with age.

→ We have used Boffi kitchens for years. They are beautiful but expensive. In order to save on costs, we always buy a floor model which is at least 50-percent less. We also have designed many kitchens with much less expensive cabinets, in which case we add more expensive hardware.

→ We used expensive tile in the master bathroom but lots of inexpensive subway tile everywhere else.

→ The lighting is a mix of vintage and modern, and both high and low end. We hung the best lighting in the main areas of the house.

The spacious kitchen with a very long island which accomodates 2 sinks.

ABOVE AND OPPOSITE: There wasn't much to salvage in this house, but we did manage to save the railing from the spiral staircase and the original details from the vaulted ceiling.

FOLLOWING PAGES: The master bedroom.

"One of the things that attracts me to vintage and antique things is **THEY HAVE STORIES**, and even if I don't know the stories, **I MAKE THEM UP.**"
—**Mary Kay Andrews**

ABOVE: The master bathroom got incredible light so we could afford to paint it black, which adds a dramatic flair to the space. We used simple black solar shades in all of the bathrooms for a clean look that matched the steel windows.

OPPOSITE: Old items like this tall candelabra from a church is a great way to display jewelry.

We carried the look of the steel framed windows to the girls' bathroom, which gives it a spa-like feel.

Every year since the girls were 8, Robert has purchased a piece of art for each of them for Christmas. There were many years that they would have preferred clothing or new iPhones, but now that they're older, they're grateful and both girls have an appreciation and growing knowledge of the world of art.

ABOVE AND OPPOSITE: Even though
this house is large, we turned the 7
bedrooms into 4, which means the
kids have to bunk together. We feel
it's important for kids to share rooms
for as long as possible—though the
kids may disagree!

We moved our 3 youngest boys into 2 adjoining rooms. They share one for sleeping and use the larger room as a playroom.

THE MUSIC ROOM

Soundproofing a room really needs to be done by a sound professional. But since we weren't going to be recording albums, we didn't want to incur that expense. We were looking for a fun music room where our kids could play instruments and be as loud as they wanted. Here's how we accomplished that:

→ Our main expense was a heavy stainless steel soundproof door. It does the job, and though it doesn't quite muffle *all* the noise, it makes it so that whatever noise does escape remains at a low, quiet tone.

→ We added extra insulation in the ceiling and the walls. A professionally soundproofed room would have required much more extensive work, including soundproofing foams and panels.

→ We built the music room on the bottom floor of the house, so that the little noise that does spill out can not be heard on the higher floors.

OPPOSITE: The music room is definitely the kids' favorite room: they can be loud and get crazy, and we don't have to know about it.

ABOVE: Another favorite room is the theater. We thought it would be a big asset for resale with a Hollywood Hills home.

OUTDOOR SPACE: WHAT WE DID

→ In addition to the hedges that we planted immediately after buying the house, we planted an additional 30 trees around the perimeter for privacy—and free fruit.

→ We incorporated sprinkler systems and great outdoor lighting everywhere, all with timers.

RIGHT: We kept the egg-shaped pool because we loved the retro style. We chose grass instead of tile because it's not so hot on the feet.

FOLLOWING PAGES: A fire feature is always a good idea. This one is particularly dramatic set inside a concrete column on the patio.

> **"**The power of imagination makes us INFINITE.**"**
>
> — **John Muir**

THE GREAT OUTDOORS

Having a big backyard was not the main reason we moved to Los Angeles but it was definitely a big reason. Coming from New York City, it felt like a real luxury for the kids to be so free and active in the outdoors. Up until this house, we'd only built and worked on rooftop gardens and small outdoor spaces but never a yard of this size. We were intimidated by how big it was and feared that we couldn't pull it off, so we met with one of the top landscape architects in Southern California. She had done one of our favorite projects of all time. Unfortunately, her bid was more than our entire budget for the complete renovation, so we decided to do it on our own.

HOW WE BUILT IT

→ We did a ton of research on outdoor space, found yards and all types of landscapes that we loved online.

→ Our goal was to keep it minimal and open so the kids would have a large area to play on.

→ We hired a local and inexpensive landscaper who drove 30 miles away to get the best and most affordable trees he could find. He had a ton of knowledge and we leaned on him for much advice throughout the project.

→ To create a more uniform look, we planted olive trees throughout. They are our favorite. We also learned the hard way they that they don't need much water.

→ We planted lemon and orange trees. We had a blast as this was something that we'd never dreamed of doing.

> **"**Should not the role of design be to RECONNECT human beings with their SPACE on their land.**"**
>
> **—Dan Kiley, landscape architect**

OUTDOOR KITCHEN: WHAT WE DID

↪ Installed a pizza oven because we love pizza.

↪ Installed a large grill because we have so many kids.

↪ Built an outdoor fireplace for chilly LA nights.

↪ Installed a beer tap, which is great for parties but dangerous for daily use!

↪ Installed two icemakers because you can never have enough ice.

↪ Added an outdoor refrigerator.

↪ Created seating for 25 because we have a big family and beer on tap.

"Creativity takes
"COURAGE"
—Henri Matisse

THE ART HOUSE

WEST VILLAGE, NEW YORK CITY

The before (ABOVE) and after (TOP) photos for this project say it all— this was one of our most ambitious projects to date.

GOALS

1 To build a large, modern home with enormous glass windows with art inside and out.

2 To create an architectural gem on Manhattan's iconic West Side Highway.

3 To design a 6-story townhouse that looks like a museum but feels like a home—tricky stuff!

CHALLENGES

→ **Building a home next to a river:** Flooding is always a concern regardless of where you are in New York City, but even more so when you build a house with the Hudson River 100 feet away. With the exception of the basketball court, we used tile over poured cement for the ground floor and the side-walls in case there was a flood. It was a wise move, as Hurricane Sandy hit a year after we moved in and it could have been catastrophic. Because of how we built the house, we had limited damage and all was restored relatively quickly.

→ **To install high-end flooring in a home with many children:** We used zebrawood floors throughout the house. Zebrawood flooring is beautiful but it's expensive and scratches way too easily, as we soon learned the hard way. The lesson: Consider how the space will be used and by whom before you make any decisions regarding flooring.

→ **To build an 80-foot-tall house from the ground up, flanked by large buildings on three sides:** Anytime we encounter structural and engineering challenges, we always devote our resources to bringing in the best engineers. This is not our expertise so we use the pros. It is not the most glamorous part of our work, but it's absolutely the most important. It doesn't matter how beautiful the building is if it collapses. Three rules for structural issues:
1. Consult an engineer.
2. Consult an engineer.
3. Consult an engineer.

→ **To install massive (20 x 12 feet) glass windows, and somehow not hear the noisy traffic below:** Soundproofing works. We originally built the windows as double-plated, but we could still hear the traffic. So we had to add a third plate to the windows to finally quell the noise at a great cost.

→ **To install an elevator *after* the house was built:** When we built the house initially, we did not install an elevator; we learned later, when it was time to put the home on the market, that this was a major mistake. We decided against an elevator because we like stairs (good exercise!), plus we had bad memories of an elevator we'd installed in a project 10 years before. It had been a huge headache and never worked properly. But we should have done our homework: in the 10 intervening years since we had installed one, house elevators had improved considerably—they were faster and more efficient.

→ **To incorporate a freestanding, stainless steel and wood staircase in the middle of the house:** The floating staircase is beautiful but it was extremely difficult and expensive to install. In retrospect, and in terms of resale value, we should have used a less expensive staircase.

→ **To build a basketball court on the first floor that would double as a playroom, an entertainment space, and a home theater:** The ceilings in the back of the home on the ground floor were incredibly high, which worked for a basketball court.

"Art is as much about design as it is art.
And design is as MUCH ABOUT ART."
—Glenn Ligon

400 West Street had many lives before we bought it: it was an S&M club, a motorcycle lot, and, when we purchased the property, it was a being used as a one-story garage. It is situated between two buildings with a third directly behind it and a highway outside the front door—which is why no there were no buyers until we came along. We saw nothing but potential. The property was deeper than anything we'd looked at in New York City. We knew that we could go higher than we had ever built, with ceiling heights and number of stories, and capture the spectacular views of the Hudson River with floor to ceiling windows on every level. We envisioned an iconic building that would stand out among the buildings along the West Side Highway.

The minute we saw it, we knew it was an opportunity to create a house where art was featured on every surface, including the facade: we commissioned Richard Woods to create an artwork for the front exterior that would stand out among some of the most incredible architecture just a few blocks from us, including buildings by Richard Meier, Jean Nouvel, and Frank Gehry.

We wanted the home to have a museum feel with stark white walls and art everywhere, but at the same time we wanted the home to feel like a haven for our large and ever-growing family. We knew that we could build for both art and function. So, we bought the lot and built the home of our dreams. Or at least the home of our dreams that year.

ABOVE AND OPPOSITE: Two views of the entryway—the two paintings on the wall are by Richard Woods, the artist who created the faux wood panel artwork for the facade.

VOLKS EN - RED - 93

SKODA . . RELIAB

THE KITCHEN: WHAT WE DID

↦ We placed the Murano chandelier over the
industrial kitchen island instead of hanging
it over the table.

↦ We installed hardwood flooring instead of tile.
The wood floors make the space feel larger
and they're just as easy to clean.

↦ The marble countertop on the island (RIGHT)
stands out, particularly since we used stainless
steel counters for the rest of the kitchen, in keeping
with the industrial feel. Employing mismatched
countertops in the kitchen helped with the cost—
we used the show-stopper material (marble) in one
location, and then less expensive options for the
rest of the space.

We believe that the kitchen table (FOLLOWING
PAGES) is the most important piece that you'll ever
purchase for your home, at least it was in our case. It's
the soul of the house and serves everyone throughout
the day: it's a place for entertaining, studying, doing
homework, building a business, gossiping, nurturing,
sharing stories, gathering, handling a crisis, celebrating,
grieving, and at the end of most days, it's where our
family connects, and checks in with one another. We
found this long zinc table at a flea market. It originally
came from a university in Paris. It's now at our home
in Massachusetts. It's one of the few items that we
will never part with. So much of our family's life has
unfolded at that table—it holds ten-thousand stories.

RIGHT: The kitchen.

FOLLOWING PAGES: We rarely
have kitchen or dining room tables
that come with a matching set of
chairs—we love the contrast this
approach creates. We encourage
our clients to do the same!

The painting of the girl in the yellow dress by Erwin Olaf is one of our favorites. It has been an anchor in every new house we've lived in since we bought it. The word painting by Graham Gilmore.

"Architecture is the thoughtful MAKING OF SPACE."
—Louis Kahn

We love to entertain and by installing a large glass garage door in the living room that adjoins the patio, we essentially merged the interior and exterior space, which allowed parties to get a whole lot bigger. We also extended the stairs that led to the door to be as wide as the house so that they could serve as stadium seating for large gatherings and performances.

We had a lot of art in this house, and it was designed with opportunities to showcase it in mind. When we began our design career and our budget was limited, we purchased a lot of art from artists on the streets of New York City. Some of it was great and some was not so great but it was our way of surrounding ourselves with art, which is something we love. As our tastes changed, we gifted much of the art to family and friends. They loved it, as not many of them had received art as present or a housewarming gift.

ART DOESN'T HAVE TO COST A FORTUNE. IT'S EVERYWHERE:

⇢ Family photographs.

⇢ Family heirlooms.

⇢ Your kid's art—add an inexpensive frame and it will instantly feel more polished.

⇢ Tag sales and flea markets are a great source for inexpensive art—and you never know, you might find a Picasso one day!

⇢ Local art fairs—we've found incredible art at fairs. And it's always a bonus to support local artists.

The master bedroom was dominated
by a massive Zaha Hadid desk and
a diminutive, though no less special,
Maarten Baas chair. Our good friend
the art dealer Kenny Schachter had
been telling us for years that Zaha
Hadid was going to be the architect
of her generation. He urged us to
purchase this incredible desk/sculpture
for the house. It was 19 feet long and
9 feet high and we needed a crane to
get it through the window frame before
we installed the glass. Years later, when
we sold the house, we also had to sell
the desk because we had no place to
store it. We were terribly sad to part
with it, as we loved the piece. But we
made a nice profit, which helped with
the separation anxiety. Kenny was
certainly correct as Hadid, who recently
passed away, will be remembered as
one of the all-time greats.

Shortly after our first TV show started airing, we were contacted by thousands of people who wanted to come to New York City to meet us and see this house in person. Mostly it was exciting and we were flattered, but it was also somewhat scary. Our kids were young and strangers were inviting themselves into our home. During this time we received several emails from a photographer named Catherine Hall. At first we disregarded them as we were overwhelmed with the attention this show brought to our family. But, after the third or fourth note from Catherine, we took a look at her work and saw that she was brilliant. We replied and soon after she began shooting our projects and our family. Ten years later she still is. She's become a dear friend and Robert was even a minister at her wedding. This is not to say that you should invite strangers into your home, but there are times when it's worth the risk.

ABOVE An indoor basketball court was definitely one of the most ambitious features of a house we've ever built. Our oldest son Wolfie is an avid basketball player and he and his friends spent many hours practicing in there.

OPPOSITE The soapstone tub is probably the most extravagant

fixture we've ever purchased for a home. At the beginning of each job we make a wish list and a budget, and this tub was at the top of the list. We'd seen it years before and dreamt of owning it one day. It's as comfortable as it looks. We still miss it. (But we still have the great piece of art that is hanging above it, *The Queen*, by Ann Carrington!)

We hang every kind of art in the kids' bedrooms—from something they've made to flea market finds to well-known artists (as long as it's framed).

We were once asked to write an article for a highbrow art magazine about how we started collecting contemporary art. Robert compared it to collecting baseball cards that he was obsessed with as a kid. He collected thousands of cards and became more knowledgeable on each player as his collection and passion grew. He learned to appreciate what it meant to actually see a Honus Wagner or a Babe Ruth card in real life. Art collecting is no different. The more you know about an artist or a period of art, the more you will appreciate it. The snobby art magazine editor thought that Robert was crazy and never printed the story as he couldn't see the parallel between a kid's collectible and high art but it was perfectly obvious to us!

OPPOSITE We rarely put designer furniture in kids' spaces for obvious reasons but this blue plastic Mark Newson chair was perfect for the boys because of its durability and playfulness.

ABOVE One of our favorite pieces that we have bought is *Self Portrait* by Vik Muniz. Muniz is known for creating masterpieces from found objects, trash, human hair, or, in this case, toys. We couldn't resist this for one of the kids' rooms.

CHAPTER THREE

THE SHARE ECONOMY

CREATING THE PERFECT AIRBNB HOUSE

GOALS

1 To turn the house into an attractive rental so that it provides an alternate source of revenue for the owner. The owner travels a lot, and he wanted to make sure he could rent the house to many types of renters— families, couples, or groups of friends.

2 To incorporate design elements and entertainment areas that would appeal to guests of all ages.

3 To bring color and light into a home set in the often-overcast Pacific Northwest, so that even on the greyest day, it will feel joyful and vibrant.

CHALLENGES

→ **To achieve a balance between function and sophistication:** We designed game and entertainment spaces throughout the house for all types of guests, but retained a sophisticated look with elements of high design so that it would not look like an activity center. We did this by using Lucite tables to hold the games, adding a gorgeous pool table, creating beautiful seating areas, and avoiding anything that could look like clutter.

→ **To create privacy within a large shared space:** Each bedroom feels like a suite, which was our goal so that guests could have their own mini-haven inside a large house.

→ **To build in inclement weather:** The home is on the Washington coast which meant contending with many rainy days while building. This had a major impact on the roof construction, the porch, the outdoor fireplace, and the rest of the exterior work. We chose materials that would work with the rain and bad weather conditions, using local wood for the deck and outdoor furniture, and we asked the locals for additional guidance.

→ **To bring the sunshine in:** As the weather is often dreary in Seabrook, we used vibrant colors throughout the home on the walls (chartreuse paint in the dining room, bold wallpaper patterns in the bedrooms) and with furnishings and other decorative elements (a pink trunk, a mint stove, yellow hooks in the mudroom, dark pink draperies, etc.).

→ **To create a home that would stand out from its look-alike neighbors:** The area is beautiful but the homes and their décor are somewhat cookie-cutter. We wanted this project to feel unique and we accomplished this by incorporating lots of color, fun textiles, unusual window treatments, and, of course, plenty of flea market finds.

We built this house from the ground up as a 3-story Craftsman style home in Seabrook, Washington. The client, who travels often, rents it out very consistently. His requirements, aside from good design, were that it be able to handle large groups of guests at one time, and have the same durability as a hotel while retaining the warmth of a family home.

The client allowed for the budget to cover good art and industrial design as long as nothing was too precious or lacked functionality or comfort. The emphasis was on creating a space where visitors could make great memories, and hopefully want to come back, especially in such a competitive rental market.

In spite of the often rainy weather, we needed to ensure that the outdoor spaces were just as well-conceived as the indoor spaces. Creating a hearth in several places was an important element on the interior and exterior, which included fireplaces and fire pits.

Whenever we work on a project, it's important to us that it feel like a reflection of not only the client but also the setting. This project was no different: In addition to our usual range of sources for furnishings (vintage shops, big box stores, etc.), we also shopped for pieces in nearby Seattle and used local artisans to build many of the outdoor pieces.

We designed this house as if we were designing a small boutique hotel so unique elements and decorating details were a guiding principle. For the living room, we used crushed velvet in rich earth tones for the upholstery on the sofa and chairs and paired it with a deep rose pink inlay trunk that functions as a coffee table. For the other rooms, bold colors (like the dining room walls) and patterns (like the bedrooms' wallpaper) kept the design high style.

To create intimacy and a sense of community in this cavernous space, we brought in arcade games, a pool table, and added seating areas for card playing and board games. We put bar stools around the kitchen counter for hanging out while people cook. And we created spaces on each floor and on the exterior for gathering so that making s'mores by the fire or listening to records in the music room could be regular occurences.

When decorating for short-term renters, the more you provide, the better the experience (rain or shine). The open floor plan meant we had room to bring in a pool table, which provides entertainment for most of the guests. We also added vintage seating that is very comfortable and a fireplace that is used most of the year. The more feminine vibe of the pink drapes complements the masculine dark wood and Art Deco lines of the pool table.

OPPOSITE TOP: We chose chartreuse for the dining room walls and it nicely offsets the dark upholstery on the chairs and window shades.

OPPOSITE BOTTOM: White subway tile never lets us down. It's classic and affordable. We love open shelving, especially in a rental—everything you need is easily in view, so guests don't have to rummage through every drawer and cupboard looking for something. We added a pop of color with the mint green stove, but otherwise used white tile and white marble countertops for a bright, clean look.

ABOVE: Sometimes having too much space is one of biggest challenges we face when designing and decorating a house. For this project, we created many small nooks and hangout spots, like this windowed corner with a bar nestled in. This Lucite and mirror bar is from the 1950s, and perfectly stores just enough bottles of wine.

The house has five bedrooms, and we decided that the décor for each would be centered around a single color to differentiate them and to make each guest feel like he or she ended up in their own special room (and it's also an easy way to remember who is staying where). We accented each bedroom with fun wallpaper, custom-made beds, colorful shades, and vintage lighting.

As we designed the bedrooms, we were inspired by our favorite hotel designers, husband-and-wife team Kit and Tim Kemp. The majority of their hotel projects are located in London (the Haymarket Hotel) and New York City (the Crosby Hotel). They are known for using lots of color and bold patterns. We get inspiration from all over the world, and hotels are always one of the first places that we look (see Chapter Eleven, *Be Boutique: Learning from Hotels*, pages 210-21 for more about hotel inspiration).

Beyond the décor for each bedroom, we also concentrated on sourcing the best bedding, as it's easily one of the most important elements in a rental home. Clean, white high-quality sheets, pillowcases, and pillows, and a fluffy white duvet are essential in creating a luxe hotel feel—and they are easy to clean with lots of bleach. Remember to keep extra sheets and pillows in the linen closet.

"Study nature, love nature,
STAY CLOSE TO NATURE.
It will never fail you."
—Frank Lloyd Wright

The outdoor deck and the patio are some of the most enjoyable spots in the house, especially when there is a fire burning in the stone hearth.

"The ache for home lives in all of us, the **SAFE PLACE** where we can go as we are and not be questioned."

—Maya Angelou

CHAPTER FOUR

THE CLASSIC TOWNHOUSE

GREENWICH VILLAGE, NEW YORK CITY

GOALS

1 To bring warmth and charm to a large, brand-new townhouse.

2 To add pops of color to a white, modern space.

3 To design a practical house for a family with kids but bring in sophistication and elegance.

CHALLENGES

→ **Making a large 6-story home feel more personal:** The clients moved from a home that they had lived in for several years. It had a rich history, but the family had outgrown it. In moving to a new house, they were concerned that the patina of time would no longer be present, but by including family pictures and heirlooms, we could accomplish this relatively quickly—these items instantly tell a story. It's important to remember to update pictures and personal items frequently: your story constantly changes as your family and your home evolve.

→ **Creating a warm and cozy atmosphere in a large open home that features lots of glass:** The key to accomplishing this was layers—layers and layers of textiles, art, and books.

→ **Decorating a house with several staircases:** We created interesting landings using objects and art to break up the many staircases in the home.

→ **To balance an elegant feel with a kid-friendly vibe:** When we design for ourselves, we create homes with the mindset that our kids are going to hang out with their friends, and we like to entertain as well, so it's important that the décor is both practical and high style. We approached this project in the same way: we designed the entertaining areas in this home for kids and adults, keeping the look sophisticated while incorporating durable fabrics and furnishings.

It's always a treat for us to take on a project like this Greenwich Village townhouse. The client had originally fallen in love with one of our homes that was on the market at the time, but she and her family preferred this location. It was new, modern, and beautifully constructed but was lacking warmth and soul.

Because the family already owned a fantastic collection of art and antiques, our job was made even easier. We have worked on projects where the clients owned objects and heirlooms that were meaningful to them but not aesthetically pleasing, so this felt like a dream. We've learned over the years that people's treasured objects are usually non-negotiable, and the challenge is creating a design and décor scheme that showcases these items, but without detracting too much from the overall vision. As with most things in life, this involves delicate negotiation.

But, for this project, no such diplomatic skills were necessary and we were able to proceed with all of our instincts. The house felt like the perfect blank canvas and we took our cue accordingly. We added lots of color with wallpaper and paint and brought in textiles, rugs, and vintage pieces for added soul, and one-of-a-kind fixtures to personalize each space. One of our signatures is incorporating truly unique and interesting lighting, and this project was no exception. Our favorite example in this house was a large Murano chandelier that had actually been in one of our homes. We purchased it in Fayence, France, 10 years earlier and it lived in our kitchen for many years. The clients saw it and asked if they could buy it from us—we were happy to oblige as we knew it would be perfect.

Perhaps one of the best parts of the job, though, was being able to showcase the family's extensive book collection. We love books—writing them, reading them, and showcasing them. And with a collection this big, it allowed us to get creative in designing custom bookshelves for each floors.

This small office on the top floor is not off-limits to kids, yet it was clearly designed for the parents. It's a space to escape the city and read a few of those books that live downstairs or to watch the sun come up. This room has access to an outdoor terrace so we used that as the theme, with lots of green notes. We brought in the client's keepsakes from Indonesia that they had collected over the years. Other highlights are the Rob Pruitt panda bear paintings and souvenirs from the client's travels abroad.

ABOVE AND OPPOSITE: The books steal the show on every floor of the house. The husband and wife are voracious readers and own a major book collection. We built custom shelving throughout the home to showcase it. We feel that books are their own form of art and they add character, personality, and soul to any space.

HOW TO CREATE CUSTOM WORD ART BOOKSHELVES

1 Before you begin, unless you are a carpenter or spend an enormous amount of time at Home Depot, we highly recommend using a skilled artisan.

2 We chose the word "EAT" as the bookshelves would be installed in the kitchen. We liked this word because each letter was rectilinear, which is better suited for creating a bookshelf.

3 We drew "EAT" on a large piece of craft paper and indicated exactly where the shelves would be installed to make sure the sizing was perfect.

4 The shelves were created from a high quality plywood because it has enough bend yet is durable and strong (and inexpensive).

5 We painted the shelves with furniture paint, using the same color throughout. By painting them dark grey, the colors of the books stand out.

6 In keeping with the theme, all the books featured are cookbooks.

CREATE A FUN CASUAL KITCHEN

→ We brought in a table large enough to accommodate the family and additional guests so that it could be used for more than just family meals. As far as we are concerned, no matter how many people live in a house, the more seats at the table the better. That way there's always room for visitors.

→ The wallpaper on the ceiling—which is striped in muted colors—is an unexpected touch.

→ The décor is simple—wood cabinetry, marble counters—so we added a major piece of art by Ann Carrington as a focal point.

→ Cookbooks of all kinds are a great way to accessorize—we use them throughout.

→ A breakfast counter with stools is always a good look, even in a kitchen with a big table.

RIGHT: The kitchen is on the ground floor and it opens up to a fantastic backyard, which is rare in New York City. Our aim was to create a kitchen that was comfortable and casual, as the home has a proper dining room for formal use.

FOLLOWING PAGES: The décor of the dining room is built around hues

of blue and various types of wood (paneling on the walls and oak flooring). The showstoppers in the room are the *VOTE* painting by Trey Speegle and the extraordinary vintage Murano chandelier hanging above a sleek, modern Kartell dining table in baby blue.

The clients had an incredible and very diverse art collection when we met them, ranging from family portraits to fun prints from their travels to a Picasso. But the space was large and had many wonderful walls that were begging for more art. We purchased work from some of our favorite artists, including Ann Carrington, Rob Pruitt, and Trey Speegle. In the sitting room with a modern fireplace, the large colorful painting is by David Kramer.

Don't forget that hallways and staircases can be places to add lots of visual interest in a home—and it's particularly unexpected to go a bit bold in these areas. The bright and cheerful wallpaper features a pattern made up of vintage book covers. To complement the contemporary staircase—with the sides painted in black sleekly emphasizing the zig-zag pattern—we added a vintage framed print, to create a bit of contrast.

There are fireplaces throughout the home, including in this master bedroom, which is a welcome and rare amenity. The contemporary glass-encased hearth beautifully shares the wall with an azure Damien Hirst painting.

Our goal was to create a sophisticated, romantic master bedroom with a soft, muted palette. To accomplish this, we used some great vintage pieces, including the client's grandmother's chair. The client's favorite artwork was by Damien Hirst, so we placed it front and center. We added sophisticated bedside tables and layered them with art books, reading lamps, and vintage lighting. The fireplace and private terrace were essential in creating the romantic vibe we were after.

For the master bathroom, the goal was a spa-like vibe. We installed marble throughout the bathroom—on the walls and countertops—and brought in a high-end tub and fixtures. We were ecstatic with the results—minimal without feeling cold, which is a delicate balance—and so were the clients.

In addition to the master bathroom, the bedroom suite also has a separate room for a vanity. Simplicity was key here as well: the custom vanity itself is a soft grey with high-end hardware, and it pairs nicely with a plush dark grey vintage rug. We added a bit of high-style drama with a gilded vintage mirror. The chair is a family heirloom which was reupholstered with a black and grey pattern. This room is one of the client's favorite spaces in the entire home. It's small, but holds her most treasured belongings. It's a place to get dressed and put on makeup but it also serves as a peaceful hideout, a place to stare out the window, meditate, or read. In keeping with Virginia Woolf's classic advice, it really is a room of her own.

MAKING A CUSTOM CHILDREN'S DESK

Believe it or not, a custom desk isn't much more expensive than a slightly pricey store-bought version, provided you're able to find a skilled carpenter.

1 We used painted MDF plywood. It is really affordable, readily available, and gives the desk a sleek look.

2 Ask your child to help with the design. You would be surprised how many great design ideas come from kids! And they will love it more because they were a part of the process.

3 No matter the ceiling height, we recommend building the desk high to use all of the space available.

ABOVE: Each of the children's bed-rooms reflects their individual personalities and different tastes, as it should be. We worked with the clients' children closely in creating their bedrooms, asking lots of questions and listening closely. We learned about their hobbies, how they use their rooms—are they extended playrooms or just a place to sleep and do homework—and their habits. The end result is a bedroom that truly functions well.

OPPOSITE: Wallpaper is used throughout the house: more classic patterns and color schemes in the main living areas, and whimsical and bold patterns in the kids' rooms. The example *par excellence* of our approach is this bedroom with an accent wall in butterfly-patterned wallpaper. It's easily one of the most joyful rooms in the house.

WALLPAPER ISN'T JUST FOR WALLS

↝ Inside the closet doors

↝ Ceilings

↝ Inside kitchen cabinets

↝ Staircases: on the riser of each step

↝ Inside bookshelves

↝ Headboards

↝ Overhead beams

" To go out with the setting sun
on an empty beach
is to truly embrace your
TUDE. "

—Jeanne Moreau

CHAPTER FIVE

THE PREFAB SURF SHACK

MONTAUK, NEW YORK

GOALS

1 To transform the generic white box prefab house into a home that that felt like it wasn't ordered from a catalogue, to give it personality and charm and make it feel like a surfing family's paradise.

2 To open up the space so that it would have an airy feel and seem larger than its 1,000 square feet.

3 To create livable outdoor space that the family could use for entertaining, eating, and hanging out.

CHALLENGES

→ **Decorating with a blueprint:** Because the home was built off-site, we didn't have the opportunity to spend time in it before we started our decorating plans, which is unusual for us. We had to rely on blueprints, the manufacturer's renderings, and extrapolate the best we could.

→ **Limited options:** Because a prefab home is built in a factory, the windows, doors, cabinets, vanities, and finishes come from a very limited list of options the client had to choose from. That made the challenge greater and put more pressure on all the choices we made for the decorating.

→ **The space felt small for 4 people:** The house was less than 1,000 square feet, and we needed it to seem larger and more open so that the family would not feel like they were on top of each other. We did this by asking the factory to make a few changes: we increased the height of the doors by a few inches, we raised the ceilings by a few feet, and removed several of the walls. This made an enormous difference in the flow of the space.

→ **Transforming a generic white box into a home:** This is a common challenge for many of the spaces we design—apartments, rentals, modular homes, etc.—but there are lots of ways to bring in charm to these kinds of spaces. In this home, because of the size, we kept the overall design minimal but used bold accents liberally in the furnishings, art, and other décor. We also brought in elements from nature and items otherwise related to the beachside setting, including the client's paddle collection and surf art.

We have designed a few spaces in the Hamptons, but Montauk has always been our favorite spot. We love the sheer beauty, laid-back vibe, and family atmosphere. In recent years, Montauk has become trendy, though, with young partiers from nearby New York City affecting the peaceful setting all summer long, bringing noise, traffic, and higher prices for everything, including real estate. To save money, our clients chose a prefab home to put on the lot they had purchased. The land was expensive but the prefab house was far more cost-efficient than building a traditional house.

The clients live in New York City and were looking for a simple escape on the beach. They are a surfing family and wanted the home to represent that. They asked that the outdoor space be as livable as the interior, and that the interior feel like them—open, warm, and relaxed.

We faced quite a few challenges with this project, chief among them being we had never designed a prefab home. While other designers work from blueprints, we were not accustomed to it—we've always worked directly inside the physical space, even if it was in the process of being transformed with a major renovation. It's hard to feel the essence or soul of a house with a set of blueprints. Because the client asked that the furniture, textiles, and décor be purchased and ready to go before the home was delivered, we did more measuring than we are used to, but went with our gut on most decisions, which paid off.

A few words to the wise about prefab houses: there are many advantages, but those need to be weighed against the disadvantages. Here's a quick list of the upsides: affordability (because they are built off-site under relatively controlled conditions), shorter construction time than a house built from the ground up, and energy efficient (they are built with airtight seams, which means that heat and cooling don't escape, helping to lower utility bills). And here are some of the downsides: preparing the land on which it will be installed (this means getting the land secured, inspected, soil-tested, and preparing the plot for sewer strikes, water, and electrical connections, not to mention obtaining the proper permits), upfront costs and payments (you must pay for it in full before they ship it to you), and transportation costs (the house will need to be shipped and though the house itself is relatively inexpensive, shipping the house to your location can add up quickly).

A view from the kitchen to the deck.

TIPS FOR BRINGING A WHITE BOX TO LIFE

→ Incorporate vintage pieces and antiques to soften the modular look. Antiques add character and warmth. They don't have to be expensive, and as long as they speak to you, they will help create a much more lived-in look. It only takes one or two pieces to change the feel of a room.

→ Wallpaper is a fast and relatively inexpensive way to transform a space. We use wallpaper in almost all of our projects.

→ Use your photos, and put them anywhere: framed on walls, on bookshelves, or collaged and printed as wallpaper (a local copy shop can often do this easily)

→ Shelving: add shelves in interesting nooks or unused spaces.

We tried something new with the sectional sofa in this house: We used different upholstery for two of the sections, and we are really happy with the results. We think the cool grey of the sofa—and the accent sections in baby blue and a striped pattern—goes perfectly with the black-and-white photo of a swimmer in a pool.

DISPLAY WHAT YOU COLLECT

A collection of almost anything can add personality to a home. The beauty of white walls is that they are a perfect backdrop for personal treasures. We learn a ton about our clients by understanding what they collect. It's one of the first things we inquire about when starting a job. Most of the time they aren't thinking about using their collections as décor, but they are always glad we did at the end of the process. Here are few suggestions about what you can use:

- Vintage quilts (in baskets or on the beds)
- Design, art, and photography books, books in general
- Family photos
- Old tickets (to anything) can be displayed in cases or in frames
- Kids' art

- Old sporting items: paddles, polo sticks, surfboards, old trophies
- Antique anything
- Toys: Pez, Bobbleheads, snow globes, comic books
- Vinyl records
- Musical instruments

We have designed a few homes for surfers, and even a hotel with a surfing theme. We've learned a lot about the lifestyle and the sport in the process (though neither of us can get on a board!). We love surf photography and art with a beachy vibe. We purchased the art for this house locally and online. A listing of our favorite websites that sell original paintings, photographs, and limited edition prints can be found in the Resources section on pages 222–23. Some of our favorite surf photographers are Tony Caramanico, LeRoy Grannis, Jeff Divine, and Clark Little.

For the boys' beds we used inexpensive frames from Ikea but we added Jonathan Adler fabric to give them a high-end look. The bright orange surfboard on the wall is a wonderful complement to the dreamy blues in the bedding.

OPPOSITE: The bedside table came from a local artisan. We try to use many local artists' and designers' work in our projects no matter where we are in the world. The easiest way to find the best local artisans and craftsmen is to ask the contractor first, as they often know who is good, what they charge, and how fast or slow they typically work.

ABOVE: The vanity was pre-ordered and installed at the factory. We added the mirrors and lighting. We chose the open space for the towels for easy access.

Knowing that the family would be spending as much time outside as they could, we designed the deck and outdoor space to function as another living area, with plenty of places to sit, hang out, play games, read, and watch the sunset over the ocean. The seating fabric for the long bench is from Maharam, which is expensive so we cut costs elsewhere, like the free surfboard coffee table made by one of the client's sons. It was the perfect touch to complete the outdoor patio.

"IT'S ALL ABOUT WHERE YOUR MIND'S AT."

— Kelly Slater

"LESS
IS
MORE."

—Ludwig Mies van
der Rohe

CHAPTER SIX

LIVING LARGE

IN A SMALL SPACE: BUNGALOW EDITION

SAN DIEGO, CALIFORNIA

GOALS

1 To create a multifunctional home in a tiny space, without skimping on style.

2 To create two sleeping areas.

3 To add storage in as many places as possible, including within the furniture.

CHALLENGES

→ **Creating a livable space in a 300-square-foot apartment:** We had to be very creative in designing a very functional layout so that every inch of it was usable.

→ **Building sufficient storage to abide by our number 1 rule for small spaces:** zero clutter.

→ **Creating sleeping areas that could be used in the daytime as well,** but did not feel like a dorm room.

→ **Finding functional and stylish furniture** that would fit down to the square inch.

→ **Transforming a very small brick patio into a chic, usable outdoor living area.** The quarters were close, but we managed to fit seating, greenery, and a fireplace.

Many manufacturers of furnishings and appliances make apartment-size versions of their full-size products. The range is a bit more limited but you always find something that fits just right, as we did with this slim-line stainless steel refrigerator.

This tiny bungalow in San Diego is the smallest home we've designed yet. The size was a bigger challenge than we had expected, not because the home was small but because of the precision required when making any choice regarding furnishings and fixtures—every measurement had to be just right, otherwise it wouldn't fit. We generally have much more leeway with our other projects.

We are familiar with living in small spaces though: When we were in-between homes, we rented a two-bedroom apartment for our family of eight. The key is zero clutter. (Of course if there are multiple people living under one small roof, the real key is getting along!)

In keeping with the zero clutter rule, we designed the bungalow to have storage in as many places as possible, including within some of the furniture.

We also chose sleeping areas that could convert to daytime use, such as a Murphy bed and convertible sofa. We aimed for the home to be as multifunctional as possible while retaining a sleek boutique look.

The home also has a cozy patio in the back. We added a seating area, a fireplace, and greenery to create an outdoor oasis/second living room, as the weather in San Diego makes it usable all year long.

We have noticed an important trend in recent years with the latest generation of home renters and buyers: They are living with less stuff and spending more of their money on travel, adventure, and experiences. It's a much wiser way to live than so many generations before them, some of whom were so attached to stuff that they seemed like borderline hoarders. Because we have moved 25 times in the last 20 years, we've had no choice other than to minimize the amount of stuff we own. Every time we move, there's a purge involved and much of what we own gets sold or given away to Goodwill or to friends. We never regret getting rid of anything and always benefit from the freedom of having done so.

In the living room, the blue sofa is a convertible and doubles as a full-size bed.

LESS IS MORE: HOW TO DECLUTTER

1 Before you begin, visualize how you want your space to look once the clutter is gone.

2 Do not purchase anything new for the space until the decluttering is done.

3 Start with the most cluttered place first. Go room by room or corner by corner.

4 Remember, it's just stuff—the most important part of any home is you and your family.

We tiled the countertops and the backsplash in crisp white square and classic subway tile in keeping with a very minimal look.

MURPHY BEDS HAVE COME A LONG WAY...

⇢ Unlike in the old days when they were made with poor quality, skinny mattresses, the new Murphy beds offer a wide range of options so you don't have to sacrifice comfort.

⇢ They aren't ugly anymore. Way back when, Murphy beds were utilitarian and that was about it. There are more options from more manufacturers these days. They now come in interesting styles and have many types of storage options.

⇢ They are easy to use. Thanks to technology, the beds store very easily and you don't have to be a body builder to operate them.

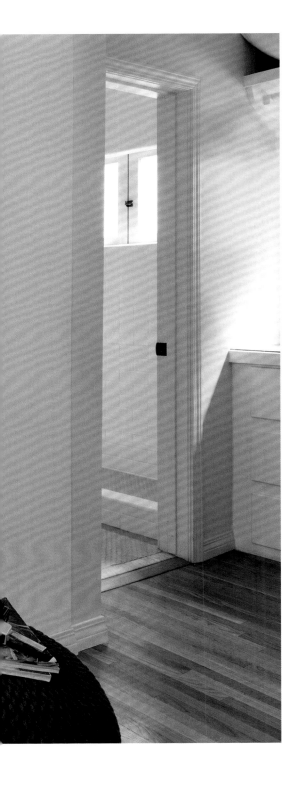

TIPS FOR A SMALL CLOSET

1 Simplify your wardrobe by donating old clothing every six months.

2 Replace closet doors with curtains.

3 Make sure you have excellent lighting—there are readily available battery-operated lights that have adhesive on the back for easy use.

4 Use a combination of hangers, shelves, boxes, and bins.

5 Boost storage power with risers and dividers.

6 K.I.S.S: Keep it simple, silly!

Outdoor space in Southern California is really an extension of the indoors, as it's used year-round. We created a second, very small living area outside with just enough furniture so that it's usable but doesn't feel too crowded. The fireplace adds color, coziness, and warmth for those chilly beach nights. It's the perfect spot for reading, napping, or sharing a bottle of wine.

"Deep summer
laziness."
RESPECT

CHAPTER SEVEN

SUMMERTIME DREAMING
THE ULTIMATE SUMMER HOME

BELLPORT, NEW YORK

GOALS

1 To bring soul to brand-new construction.

2 To create multiple entertaining spaces indoors and outdoors.

3 To incorporate antique architectural pieces from all over the world into the décor.

4 To use multiple types of wood that complement each other.

CHALLENGES

The new construction felt sterile: The home needed warmth and soul. We did this by incorporating the client's large-scale vintage architectural and decorative elements—like screens, door frames, etc.—as well as fabrics, antiques, family heirlooms, and old paintings so that the new home would feel lived-in.

Bringing nature indoors: We wanted to honor the landscape and beauty that surrounds the house and do so in a way that flowed with the design and construction. To accomplish this, we brought in large trees and used them as decorative columns. We also added wood paneling throughout the house.

Serving the needs of a large family that entertains: The client asked that we make the house feel like a family home with areas for everyone to have their own space but also accommodate larger groups when they entertain. To do that, we created one large open space for the dining room, living room, and kitchen, and created more intimate spots elsewhere by adding seating areas to the oversize hallways and bedroom suites.

Maintaining privacy without obstructing the views: In some cases, we opted for window treatments, while in other parts of the house we used screens and dividers.

Timing and coordination while collaborating with the local architect and landscape architect: We made this work through communication, respect and ... more communication.

A fun New York City family that we'd known for years asked us to help them create their dream summer home in the tony town of Bellport, Long Island. The project was a collaboration between a local architect, a landscape designer, and us. The goal was to design and build a spectacular new home but to bring in character and soul, so it felt as though the family had lived there for a long time. There's always a bit of risk when there are so many chefs in the kitchen, so to speak, but in this case it worked out well because of good communication and the creative team putting their egos aside in service of the client.

We aren't purists in our décor (or otherwise!) and we certainly don't follow very many rules, so when the client asked us to incorporate huge architectural pieces from their travels around the globe into brand-new construction, we got excited. We fully believe that if you love something—no matter how unusual, no matter how much it doesn't "go"—you can make it work in your décor. That was the overarching theme of this project— incorporating seemingly disparate elements and furnishings that the family loved and treasured, including heirlooms, antiques, photos, and art.

The fabric on the bench belonged to the client's late mother. The client asked that we find a way to incorporate it into the design, so we reupholstered the kitchen banquette with it—that way, her mother would always have a seat at the table.

OPPOSITE AND ABOVE: The kitchen décor was relatively simple with a few pops of color: marble countertops and white cabinetry with a sea blue backsplash and bright accents like a sunshine yellow teapot and cake stand.

FOLLOWING PAGES: We added the shimmering white and purple wallpaper because, well, the client loves purple and asked if we'd use it throughout the home. We love that color, too, but it's not an easy color to work with. To tone it down and incorporate it into the rest of the design, whites and neutrals were a must. The white kitchen table brings this space together and allows the purple and other vibrant colors to work their magic.

OPPOSITE: In spite of this room being the formal dining room, we wanted the vibe to be casual yet polished. The salvaged wood table and wood wall paneling are nicely accented by bright blue wicker chairs.

ABOVE LEFT: The clients purchased the intricate archway in Bali while on their honeymoon 20 years earlier. We

used it as a frame for the entryway to the family room. We have been incorporating salvaged architectural elements into our work since our earliest projects—we've used salvaged windows, columns, doors, and floors from old buildings, churches, and hospitals.

ABOVE RIGHT: Bellport is cold in the winter and has many chilly nights

even in summer, so the fireplace is a much-used feature. We worked with local artisans to create the slate hearth with exposed storage for logs.

ABOVE: There were trees that had to be removed from the property, so it made sense to incorporate them into the house somehow. We worked with the landscape architect to identify which trees were best for this purpose. We prepared them by stripping the bark, sanding them down, and adding a sealant. This transformed the old trees into these stunning decorative columns. We found the vintage lights at an antiques store, painted them in varying shades of purple and blue and hung them at different heights in the stairwell between the trees.

OPPOSITE: We chose not to do any drapes in the living room because the house looks out onto the bay. Privacy was unnecessary and the views were too good to obstruct. The seating area is grounded by one of our favorite rugs that we designed for our own line—it spells out "FAMILY" in large letters.

OPPOSITE: A room with a view—this seating area is complete with high-end rattan chairs and a diminutive table nestled next to a bank of windows.

ABOVE: Though the client's favorite color is purple, she was open to bringing in color of all shades as evidenced by this serene hallway in seafoam blue with 2 tall turquoise vases and vintage crystal ceiling lights from Canopy Designs.

TIPS FOR A BETTER MAN CAVE

1 Think Ralph Lauren not TGI Fridays.

2 Comfortable seating is absolutely key but don't resort to a La-Z-Boy—
   there are lots of options for stylish and comfortable seating.

3 Don't allow the television to take over the space.

4 Add mementos and awards from the glory days. They are a fun way
   to personalize the space.

5 Vintage pennants, photos, and sports memorabilia can be found at flea
   markets and tag sales. You can even pick up a couple of old trophies,
   just in case you never won any yourself.

6 A vintage pinball machine or arcade game is a plus.

The husband asked us to design a
man cave so that he'd have his own
private space within the house. We
designed a room for him that feels
like an escape—with his collectibles
on display—but is still connected to
the rest of the décor of the house.

OPPOSITE: The master bathroom is a blend of old and new. The wainscoting ceiling brings a feeling of the past while the blue mosaic tiles add a bright, contemporary touch.

ABOVE: We used shades of blue throughout to play off the waterside setting; it also tones down the formality while adding a beach feel to the home. The mirrored screen is also from the clients' travels in Bali.

TIPS FOR PHOTO WALLPAPER

- Digital printing companies who can produce it are easy to find online. In New York, we work with Duggal.
- The more images the better.
- The strongest images should be the largest and placed toward the center of the layout.
- High-resolution images are a must.

ABOVE: Kids' rooms are always fun to design. The teenage daughter has eclectic tastes and the result was a mix of antiques, bold colors, and quirky elements like the swing. She also selected the images for the photo wallpaper to create an accent wall behind her bed.

OPPOSITE TOP: For the 10-year-old daughter's bedroom, we used mosquito nets that we brought back from Brazil and added a custom pom-pom border around the edges to personalize them.

OPPOSITE BOTTOM: We aimed to make the guest room bright, bold, and full of life. The accent wall features a red and blue floral wallpaper which is set off by the simple dresser in primary red.

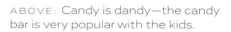

ABOVE: Candy is dandy—the candy bar is very popular with the kids.

RIGHT: The media room is our favorite room in the house. The client allocated a big part of the budget for the magnificent Roche Bobois sectional, which instantly made the space fun, colorful, and comfortable. The sectional also makes the room easy to reconfigure depending on how many people are using it.

"What I wanted to do was to paint **SUNLIGHT** on the side of a house."

—Edward Hopper

CHAPTER

HOME REDUX

REFRESHING A COUNTRY HOME

GREAT BARRINGTON, MASSACHUSETTS

GOALS

1 To add a large mudroom to the front entrance of the house.

2 To renovate the attic and create an additional sleeping area.

3 To update all the lighting.

CHALLENGES

→ **To build a mudroom without spending a fortune:** We had to figure out how to add the mudroom without adding an extra roofline. The front porch was the best place to make this happen. Before the mudroom, we had many hooks and a freestanding coat rack, neither of which were enough to hold all our coats and gear. It got especially chaotic when we had guests, as the coat rack would often collapse under the weight of coats.

→ **To create a functional room in the attic with very low ceilings:** The big challenge with the attic renovation was the low ceiling height. We kept the beams exposed to gain as much space as possible. We also left the electrical boxes exposed and resting on the beams to save headroom. (Normally there would be dry wall around the electrical box.) We painted the entire attic white, including the floors, to make it feel larger and more open. Our kids now play up there for hours. It also comes in handy for sleepovers; we can fit a lot of kids up there.

Like most New Yorkers, and indeed everyone across the country, we were profoundly affected by September 11, 2001. After that tragic day, many New Yorkers either felt a need to move away from the city entirely or to at least find a place to retreat to, a second home, a place that felt far away from the hell of what we had just experienced. We did the latter.

We wanted an inexpensive house in a small town, a place in or near nature, where our city kids could play on grass and dirt and roam free. It wasn't long before we found the town and the home that felt perfect for our family: Great Barrington, Massachusetts. We paid very little for the house because it was in terrible shape, but we thought it had great bones and we fell in love with the huge yard and the gorgeous trees surrounding it.

Though we are constantly moving—renovating and then selling our houses—this home is different. We will own this house forever—it's our family home. And it's also our design laboratory in many ways. We've been there for almost two decades and have renovated, revamped, and restyled it many times over the years. It has grown and evolved with our family, and truly holds the story of us within its old country walls.

While we have included this home in other books, it has changed so much over the years. We thought it would be good to show the changes we have made recently: the mudroom, redoing the window treatments (which made a big difference in the feel of the rooms), and redoing the attic to make it a livable space. This chapter is about the "refresh," about making something old new again, and about the ongoing story that a single house can tell.

While much has changed with the house, a few things have and will always remain the same: It's not and never was precious. It's well designed with fun art and furniture, but it's durable, kid-friendly, and extremely cozy. We are fortunate that it gets great light, which was one of the many reasons we bought it. The white floors make it even brighter and the open floor plan, which we use in many of our projects, is also a great feature. One of the first things we did when we started on the renovation was to knock out the walls. The open space gives the house a loftlike feel. And though the walls and flooring in the main living areas tend to be white, pops of color abound. The colors have changed over the years, but there will always be art, interesting textiles, and great furniture that bring color and happiness to every room in the home.

Both of us were raised by mothers who redecorated their homes on a yearly, and sometimes even monthly, basis. They also added on rooms as their families expanded. We grew up thinking that this zany lifestyle was normal. When we bought the house, we had 4 kids. Within a few years, we had 7. During the time we have owned it, we have repainted most of the rooms at least once and even changed our famed yellow shutters to a pale pink. We turned the simple attic into a fun sleeping loft for the kids and guests. After many years of thinking about it, we finally built a mudroom, which stores all of our ski gear and jackets. We have plans to turn the garage into more sleeping areas because all of the kids are getting bigger and one day will have kids of their own.

Years ago, while looking at a shelter magazine, we saw a ship lamp in the home of a famous designer. We loved it and spent the next several years on the hunt for something similar. Finally, in the back of a lighting store in Austin, Texas, we found what we were looking for. It was broken and missing parts, but we were elated anyway. The owner of the store told us that he'd found it in Paris and on his next trip, he'd look for the missing parts. He asked us to give him six months. Three years later, he shipped the parts to us. It was worth the wait.

BENEFITS OF A MUDROOM

- ↦ A mudroom is a great place to hang coats and store things that you don't want brought into the house, and to leave shoes in so they don't bring the outside into the home.
- ↦ It can provide a second means of egress into the house, making it safer.
- ↦ It adds a buffer between the home's interior and the cold weather.
- ↦ It makes the house more elegant. In our case, it created an entry between the front door and the living area.

OPPOSITE: The mudroom complete with lots of hooks and a bench with open storage. Originally, the front door of the house opened right into the living room, making it feel less formal, and allowing cold air to waft into the house every time someone opened the door (which happens about every 5 minutes when you have 7 kids). And because there was nowhere else to hang coats and store shoes, boots, and sporting equipment, the living room often resembled the entrance to a store. In other words, the mudroom was long overdue.

FOLLOWING PAGES: A quasi music room on the ground floor has a vintage turntable, a piano, lots of fashion and art books, and a couple of simple but comfortable chairs to read them in.

KATE MOSS

"THE BEST ROOMS HAVE SOMETHING TO SAY
ABOUT THE PEOPLE WHO LIVE IN THEM."
—David Hicks

THE ATTIC: WHAT WE DID

→ Replaced the trap door ladder with proper stairs.
→ Painted the entire space white, making it feel larger and more open.
→ Added heating and air units.
→ Placed the beds in the areas where the ceiling is the lowest.
→ Moved the majority of the kids' toys and clutter from downstairs to the attic.

PREVIOUS PAGES: The main hall-way on the second floor is hung top to bottom with family photographs. To make sure the effect wasn't too cacophonous, we converted the images to black and white.

ABOVE AND OPPOSITE: Two views of the attic—the sleeping area and seating area, both coordinated in shades of gold.

One of the best decisions we made in this house, which has stood the test of time, is to paint the bedroom walls in vibrant colors. So take it from us: don't be afraid of color! And while we were happy with that aspect of the bedrooms, we did want to make some small improvements, which we accomplished by changing the curtains and window shades. The treatments before were a bit more shabby chic style and we wanted something more polished. We chose bold patterns that made the rooms look fresh and new.

TIPS ON CHOOSING WINDOW TREATMENTS

1 Before you begin, determine how you are going to live in the space: Do you have children and how will they use the space? Do you like more formal living spaces or casual? Do you entertain often? These questions will help guide you as you choose the style of the shades or window treatments throughout.

2 Every room has a personality. Drapes are better for formal rooms, whereas shades are great in less formal spaces like the kitchen and kids' rooms.

3 Use a window treatment professional. Retailers like the Shade Store will come to you for free and measure your windows. We highly recommend it.

4 Blackout shades work wonders in the bedroom, but are not necessary in the main living areas.

CHAPTER NINE

APARTMENT IN THE SKY

"And you have to remember that I came to America as an immigrant. You know, on a ship, through the Statue of Liberty. And I saw that skyline not just as a representation of steel and concrete and glass, but as really the substance of the

AMERICAN DREAM."

—Daniel Libeskind

GOALS

1 To add a bit drama and elegance to a generic apartment.

2 To create an oasis in the sky for a couple who likes to entertain.

CHALLENGES

➻ **Creating lots of storage in a small apartment:** We wanted to maintain a very sleek and elegant feel, while making sure we had plenty of storage for the clients' belongings. We accomplished this by creating built-ins and added hideaway storage solutions throughout the space.

➻ **A dark bathroom:** In keeping with the dark tones of the finishes and wall treatments in the apartment (dark wood cabinetry and paneling, black marble countertops, etc.), the clients wanted to bring black tones into the bathroom, which is an unusual request. Luckily, the bathroom had a window so the natural light helped considerably.

➻ **Designing in a city known for its overwhelming building codes and mandates:** Anyone who has ever built or designed anything in New York City knows that it's very difficult. There is usually only one or two elevators in a building that can be used at certain times of the day and only during the weekdays. Then you have to contend with building managers, tenant committees for approvals, and neighbors who are really unhappy there is a construction zone across the hallway. Our advice: follow the rules so you don't have to tangle with the building management, give your neighbors a heads-up, and if someone complains, drop off a bottle of wine.

A spectacular view of New York Harbor from the dining room.

The clients asked us to completely overhaul the design of an apartment with very little charm, which is a common directive from our clients. They were incredibly enthusiastic about our ideas, which we developed in close collaboration with them. We had an ample budget allocated for furniture, which is always a plus.

Living in a small apartment is like living on a boat: every square inch must be functional because space is at a premium. Our task was to create a sleek modern design that also accommodated lots of storage, which we accomplished with built-ins.

The apartment gets incredible light, which is a rarity in New York. Having nearly floor-to-ceiling windows in much of the living spaces makes quite an impression, but it also means that the window treatments become even more important. In this apartment, privacy was less of an issue than controlling the amount of sunlight that streamed in. Further intensifying the effect of the light is the fact that the apartment overlooks the harbor. With that much direct and reflected light coming in, you are in danger of damaging artwork, rugs, and furniture through fading. Not to mention that controlling the temperature inside the apartment becomes difficult—that many windows will heat up your home in the summer and, if the windows are not properly insulated, leave you cold in the winter. Blackout shades or curtains are a must.

The client allocated very little in the budget for art and instead focused their resources on exquisite furnishings. The dining table is by Collection Particulière. The vintage chairs were purchased on 1stDibs, one of our favorite online resources. If you're patient and look often enough, you can find amazing antiques online. The long tubular light is from Roll & Hill.

The client had a very expensive sectional and, in fact, we'd fantasized about owning the very same one for years. It was always out of our budget and our kids would have destroyed it. The fun part of designing other people's spaces is that you can live vicariously through their excellent design choices!

HOW TO FIND THE PERFECT SECTIONAL

1 Take pictures of your space and measure before purchasing a sectional, as they tend to take up more space than you realize.

2 Think about how your other furnishings will function with an irregular-size sofa, in particular the coffee table and nearby chairs. Will you be tripping over other furniture to accommodate the sofa?

3 Modular furniture: A sectional that you can add to is a great choice for a growing family.

4 Remember style is important, but comfort is king—always test out the furniture before you buy.

TIPS FOR A BREAKFAST BAR

→ Great stools make the bar.

→ We always recommend if you're using marble or marble slab to inspect each piece *before* it's delivered. Some come with lots of grains or cracks, and other imperfections. Buyer beware.

→ Splurge on the faucet and hardware—it may seem like an unnecessary indulgence but high-end fittings and hardware can truly transform a bar, kitchen, or bathroom. For this bar, we installed a copper sink, and it was gorgeous when paired with the dark marble counters.

→ Keep appliances and other items to a minimum. Add one or two beautiful appliances and very little else.

ABOVE AND OPPOSITE: Installing a kitchen with black counters and dark cabinetry was the client's choice because she loved the elegant feel. We were initially hesitant as we normally opt for a white kitchen, for ourselves and our clients. But in this space, the dark colors weren't too heavy or ponderous because of so much natural light.

ABOVE: Expensive beds can be a very good investment. We'd rather see people spend more on their bedding and do custom beds because we spend one-third of our lives in bed. In this bedroom, the custom bedding is from Coraggio with Holland and Sherry fabric.

OPPOSITE: The extraordinary custom wood paneling and finishes in the apartment are from Henrybuilt, a New York City–based firm.

" IF A BUILDING BECOMES ARCHITECTURE, THEN IT IS ART. "

—Arne Jacobsen

ABOVE: The fantastic two-sided fire-place was designed by Echo Smart. The black-and-white photograph of Penelope Cruz is the only piece of art in the entire apartment, as the client wanted the architecture and the views to be the main focus.

OPPOSITE: A view of the living room from the bedroom.

DESIGN A BATHROOM STEP BY STEP

1 We make decisions about the tile as the first step—all other decisions fall in line after that. When the tile is installed, make sure it's properly pitched to drains and is waterproof.

2 Lighting is important, especially if your tile or other finishes are dark, and of course it's essential around the mirror.

3 Sinks, tubs, and fixtures: We've generally been opposed to very expensive sinks and tubs—we prefer to spend more money on the hardware. We also opt for separate showers and tubs, whenever possible.

4 Mirrors and accessories, such as towel bars: Mirrors come in all shapes and sizes these days. Some are really bright. Some are not so bright. As we all get older, we tend to look better in the not-so-bright ones.

Designing this bathroom was incredibly fun. We installed a whimsical Pierre Frey wallpaper and Bower Studios mirror over the vanity.

"It bothers me when people disparage
Los Angeles. They say that they
miss the culture of New York and that
New York is so stimulating.
Well, I say if you're not dull yourself,
you'll find it just as
stimulating here."

—George Cukor

CHAPTER TEN

HIS AND HERS: BLENDING STYLES

SILVER LAKE, LOS ANGELES

GOALS

1 To blend a couple's individual design ideas and styles to create a warm, inviting home.

2 To create multiple outdoor areas in spite of modest deck and patio space.

3 To create a home that was multifunctional and adaptable as the client's family grew.

CHALLENGES

→ **Making a small house feel more expansive:** The home was small, and we wanted to avoid decorating with too many furnishings, otherwise it would feel cluttered. And particularly since we were bringing together decorative elements of varying styles, we wanted the result to feel streamlined.

→ **Creating an office that could double as a guest room:** This meant that the desk setup could not be too overpowering in the room, otherwise when guests slept there it wouldn't feel very inviting. To do so, we went with a sleeper sofa, and made the desk area minimal, open, and light.

→ **To bring personality to a white box:** Our perpetual design challenge in so many of our projects is bringing warmth and personality to cookie-cutter new construction. The couple had plenty of personality, which was well-represented in the design items they already owned, and it was up to us to carry that through the rest of the design decisions in the house.

We were asked to design a home for a young couple who'd recently left their apartment in Brooklyn and headed west to Los Angeles. They decided to settle in Silver Lake, a neighborhood a few miles east of Hollywood. The funny thing about Silver Lake is that it feels more like Brooklyn than it does most neighborhoods in LA, as it's a mecca for hipsters and creatives, with a plethora of indie stores, chic boutiques, street art, artisanal coffee shops, and trendy bars and restaurants. What makes it very different from Brooklyn is the landscape and natural beauty that surrounds it. Silver Lake is set among stunning hills, with long, winding streets and grassy parks. The clients wanted their home to play off the beauty of the landscape of the neighborhood, and at the same time be a representation of them. Like many couples, they came to the project with their own set of likes and dislikes when it came to furnishings and design. Our job was to combine their two perspectives in one cohesive design scheme.

A signature aspect of our style is that we always mix and combine décor of varying styles from different periods—that always adds texture and visual interest to any room. If things are too matchy-matchy, it tends to be very boring. What we did know going into this project is that we wanted to dig deep into mid-century design as a foundation for the decorating, which is what Silver Lake is known for.

The kitchen has large windows and leads to one of the decks, so with that much sunshine coming in we knew we could install dark wood cabinetry and shelving without the space feeling dreary at all.

→ **Know thyself:** Before you begin, it's most helpful to know and understand what *you* like, and what speaks to *you* in terms of décor. With that information in hand, negotiating how the decorating scheme will come together should go more smoothly.

→ **Communicate:** Talk through what is important to each of you, and share your visions with one another from the start. As simple and obvious as this sounds, many people don't do it.

→ **Deal breakers:** Early on, share your non-negotiables with one another. It will save a lot of pain and resentment later.

→ **Telling your story:** As you begin this process, take a look at the items you are bringing together for the house—the furnishings, the art, and the décor. Decide whether or not they truly reflect you and your story—if they don't, get rid of them.

→ **Compromise and have fun:** The more you compromise and attempt to understand and embrace your partner's taste and style, the happier you will both be.

A vignette in the living room, a mix of "his" and "hers" design objects: his mid-century modern avocado green chair and the hand sculpture pair well with her vintage map on the wall and biomorphically shaped mirrors on the column.

OPPOSITE: The striped wallpaper in the dining room adds depth to the small space while creating a fun backdrop for the mid-century table and chairs.

FOLLOWING PAGES: In the office/ guest room, the white metal desk is from West Elm—we like the clean, modern lines and the wheels add flexibility. The black chair in a more traditional shape is Novogratz for CB2, and the shades are our design as well, Novogratz for the Shade Store. Just about everything else was purchased at a flea market.

The small room off the main floor needed to serve several purposes—office, guest room, future nursery—and the clients asked that it be happy and bright. Even though the room was small, we wanted to make a big statement, so we chose the turquoise wall because it's calming but also adds a fun pop of life to the space. We usually go with a less-is-more approach with bright paint and opt for an accent wall rather than painting the entire room.

We brought in a small sleeper sofa and some good but basic, big box store furnishings and styled them with personal items and quirky one-of-a-kind flea market finds to bring this room to life. We wanted the room to feel eclectic but also tell the owners' story. An extra room provides an opportunity to bring in all the things that speak to you and allows you to showcase them without feeling like you're overtaking the main living area.

We chose lightweight furniture to ensure the room was as flexible as possible (i.e., in case the clients need to quickly and easily turn it into a guest room), like the wire book shelves and a desk on wheels. We added storage without using too much space. The room gets a tremendous amount of sunlight so the patterned blackout shades were a must.

ABOVE AND OPPOSITE: Mirrors in interesting shapes are placed throughout the home, and we loved the set of triangular ones for the office/guest room. For the rug, we chose a multicolor theme with a Southwest vibe.

OPPOSITE AND ABOVE: The bathroom, with an open shower, is light and bright with floor-to-ceiling marble. In the master bedroom, we reupholstered the bed frame in a neutral, textured fabric which sets off the tapestry well.

TIPS FOR DESIGNING A DECK

→ Plan for your lifestyle: is it going to be an outdoor living room, a place to grill and dine alfresco, a party spot? Assess your needs before purchasing furniture.

→ Focus on the views: Organize the seating areas to take best advantage of whatever beauty surrounds the space.

→ Include as many plants, small trees, and other greenery as you can fit.

→ Add pattern, color, and texture to the benches, tables, and chairs with pillows, throws, cushions, and even outdoor rugs.

→ Lighting is key. Task lighting is great for walkways and entrances, outdoor pendants, and solar string lights are perfect for ambience, and it doesn't hurt to add floodlights for security.

The home has two large outdoor spaces, one in the front (right) and one in the back (see pages 192–93). The goal was to make both spaces as inviting as possible so that they would be extensions of the interior.

BE
BOUTIQUE
ING FROM HOTELS

LOBBY IDEAS TO STEAL

⇢ If you have a large open space, which can feel a bit impersonal, the idea is to divide and conquer: find a way to break down the space into more intimate seating or activity areas. And be sure to use a rug to define and separate these areas of a room.

⇢ An accent wall is a great way to highlight a feature or area of a room, or disguise an element that you don't like. In the lobby of the Hotel Dylan, it was the former: the raised platform fireplace and the chimney column were a terrific feature that we high-lighted with loden green paint and white neon wall art.

Over the past few years, we've had the privilege of designing a few boutique hotels. This had always been a dream of ours. Long before we were ever asked to do these projects, boutique hotels had served as a huge source of inspiration in our design work, and we'd been incorporating many of the ideas we'd seen into the homes we built. We feel that boutique hotels offer some of the best design ideas and decorating concepts we've seen anywhere in the world.

Many boutique hotels have mastered the art of living well in small spaces, where a single room can serve many functions, much in the same way that every home has that one room that anchors the entire house—it's the room where everything happens. For the boutique hotels we design, we put this mission into overdrive and create a space to eat, drink, retreat, read, revitalize, work, enterain, and sleep.

OPPOSITE AND ABOVE: The lobby and one of the guest rooms in the Hotel Dylan, in Woodstock, New York. Paul, the owner of the hotel, is truly our favorite client of all time; he's probably the nicest guy on the planet. We had a vision that he believed in from the start, so didn't micromanage us or the process which is rare in this business. Our advice to anyone who hires a designer: once you hire a professional you trust, let them work their magic.

ABOVE AND OPPOSITE: A few of our favorite things at the Hotel Dylan: we added feathers to simple clear glass vases to bring a sense of playfulness to each room (an inexpensive but unique touch). We used velvet chairs in interesting shapes and styles and installed different wallpaper in each room.

BATHROOM IDEAS TO STEAL

⇢ Bold paint colors in geometric patterns make a big impact in small spaces.

⇢ Mix and match styles: We use modern sinks, but the rustic table adds warmth.

⇢ Black tile is unexpected and wears well in public spaces.

⇢ An interesting mirror defines a space.

⇢ Modern hanging sinks are perfect when space is at a premium.

ABOVE AND OPPOSITE: We chose
relaxed, playful designs for the
bathrooms in the Hotel Dylan.
Bathrooms are an easy place to
take risks, whether it be unexpected
tiles, bold wallpaper, over-the-top
mirrors, or fun lighting.

TIPS ON INSTALLING SWINGING CHAIRS

1 Make sure that the ceiling can hold the weight before you install.

2 Find and mark the stud in the ceiling.

3 Drill a hole for the eye hook and screw the eye hook into the hole.

4 Loop the metal link into the eye hook.

5 Repeat tip #1!

6 Hang the chair and enjoy countless hours of relaxation.

ABOVE: We love vintage movie and music posters. We usually find them on eBay or at flea markets. You'd be surprised by what $100 gets you and we've found some gems for far less than that. Readymade frames are very reasonable and come in such a wide range of colors and styles. The faux fur pillow and throw instantly elevate a simple black chair and give it a swanky feel.

OPPOSITE: Swinging chairs—one of the best things from the '70s—bring a lot of joy to any room. They are easy to find online, too, either vintage or new. Great design ideas never die.

MUST-HAVE ALBUMS FOR EVERY VINYL COLLECTOR

We have put together several vinyl record collections for hotels. If you are just starting out, we recommend buying 20 albums to get your collection going.

1 Bruce Springsteen, *Born to Run*

2 The Beatles, *Abbey Road*

3 Beach Boys, *Pet Sounds*

4 Van Morrison, *Astral Weeks*

5 Fleetwood Mac, *Rumors*

6 Joni Mitchell, *Blue*

7 Carole King, *Tapestry*

8 Eagles, *Hotel California*

9 Simon and Garfunkel, *Bridge Over Troubled Water*

10 Stevie Wonder, *Songs in the Key of Life*

11 Neil Young, *Harvest*

12 Johnny Cash, *At Folsom Prison*

13 The Smiths, *The Queen is Dead*

14 John Coltrane, *A Love Supreme*

15 Miles Davis, *Kind of Blue*

16 Rolling Stones, *Some Girls*

17 Bob Dylan, *Blonde on Blonde*

18 Radiohead, *Kid A*

19 Led Zeppelin, *Physical Graffiti*

20 Public Enemy, *It Takes a Nation of Millions to Hold Us Back*

ART RESOURCES

Art is, and always has been, an important part of our home designs, regardless of budget. Luckily buying art for your home is easier than ever. There are plenty of sources online at every price point for everything from paintings to prints.

1stdibs.com: You can get some of the most amazing antiques in the world on this site and, yes, you can get great art there too. We purchased several pieces for clients and ourselves at bargains prices.

Artnet.com: You can bid on paintings, prints, photographs and more by the world's most sought-after artists.

Etsy.com: We love Etsy for all things collectible and crafty, and amazing art is no exception.

SaatchiArt.com: Buy some of the world's most famous artists weekly starting at 500 dollars. Their mantra is "be original, buy original," which we love.

YardDog.com: If you like outsider art or folk art check out Yard Dog, a gallery based in Austin, Texas, which has a robust website.

Once you have the art in hand, here are some tips on how to frame and display it:

- Frames ideally should be hung at eye level, not too high and not too low, about 57 inches "on center," which means the middle point of the work is 57 inches above the ground. This is the standard measurement all major museums and galleries use so you know it's right!

- When hanging a picture above a table, leave 4 to 8 inches of space between the bottom of the picture frame and the top of the table. When the piece is too close it looks too busy.

- For pieces above furniture, go 3 to 6 inches higher than the furniture (other than a table).

- Try to avoid hanging your artwork in direct sunlight. The purpose of framing art is to make it look nice and protect it, and sunlight and moisture are detrimental to this. Though we sometimes throw caution to the wind and use photos in our beach projects, it's important to remember that salty beach air is not good for photography.

- Place your framing wire as close to the top of the picture frame as you can. Doing this helps keep your picture flat against the wall by raising the picture's center of gravity.

- Use picture hanging strips that keep the frames from moving and shifting around—we use them all the time.

AIRBNB TIPS

More and more, our clients are using their homes as a second source of income by doing short-term rentals through Airbnb and similar services (see Chapter Three). We also rent our country house in Great Barrington, Massachusetts (see Chapter Eight). We have learned a lot over the years about how to create a great experience for guests and we've gathered a few tips and suggestions here.

HOW TO KEEP GUESTS COMING BACK...

- Welcome your guests with a gift basket or a bottle of booze and fresh flowers on the table.
- A guidebook for the area with places to go/things to do, with notes about your favorite places.
- Provide a list of good restaurants and delivery menus.
- Make sure the house has plenty of entertainment options (streaming services), with a smart TV and sound system: Netflix, Amazon Prime, and Spotify are among the favorites.

WHAT TO HAVE, ROOM BY ROOM

KITCHEN

- Fully stocked pantry, which includes: oil and vinegar, spices and seasonings (salt, pepper, etc.), sweeteners (sugar and sugar substitutes), coffee, and tea (black and herbal).
- Open shelving for easy access.
- A stocked bar goes a long way (provided you've accounted for these extras in your rental fee): vodka, rum, tequila, beer, and wine.

DINING ROOM

- Big, durable table for lots of guests—the more the merrier.
- No rugs—much easier to clean wood or tile floors.

LIVING ROOM

- Cozy (soft fabrics and plush cushions), over-size furniture that will wear well—dark colors in high-performance fabrics.
- Great reading material, including current magazines, popular novels (look at the *New York Times* bestseller's list for suggestions), and great coffee table books—think hotel lobby not family den.
- Provide board games and a deck of cards.

BEDROOM

- Reading lights on the night tables.
- Throw blankets, which are nice for decoration but also provide extra warmth on cold nights.
- Make sure to empty the drawers and almost all the closets—keep one closet in the house locked with a key for personal items.

A big thanks to all of the photographers who have shot our projects over the years
and whose work is included in this book:
Matthew Williams, Costas Picadas, Staci Marengo, and Luc Roymans.

—ROBERT AND CORTNEY

First published in the United States of America in 2020 by
Rizzoli International Publications, Inc.
300 Park Avenue South
New York, NY 10010
www.rizzoliusa.com

Copyright © 2020 Robert and Cortney Novogratz

Publisher: Charles Miers
Editor: Isabel Venero
Design: Kayleigh Jankowski
Production Manager: Barbara Sadick
Managing Editor: Lynn Scrabis

All rights reserved. No part of this publication
may be reproduced, stored in a retrieval system,
or transmitted in any form or by any means,
electronic, mechanical, photocopying, recording,
or otherwise, without prior consent of the publishers.

Printed in Italy

2020 2021 2022 2023 / 10 9 8 7 6 5 4 3 2 1

ISBN: 978-0-8478-6700-4
Library of Congress Control Number: 2019953585

Visit us online:
Facebook.com/RizzoliNewYork
Twitter: @Rizzoli_Books
Instagram.com/RizzoliBooks
Pinterest.com/RizzoliBooks
Youtube.com/user/RizzoliNY
Issuu.com/Rizzoli